$$\boxed{\textit{The Classic Collection}}$$

·FUN FAMILY·
FOOTWEAR

By The Staff of WORKBASKET Magazine

KC PUBLISHING, INC.

700 West 47th Street, Suite 310 • Kansas City, Missouri 64112

COPYRIGHT 1995 KC PUBLISHING, INC.

Instructions have been carefully checked for accuracy. The publisher, however, cannot be responsible for human error, misinterpretation of directions or the differences of individual needleworkers.

Attention Schools and Business Firms:
KC PUBLISHING books are available at quantity discounts for bulk purchases for education, business or sales promotion use. For more information call our Book Department at (816) 531-5730.

Printed in the United States of America

Library of Congress Cataloging-in-Publication Data

FUN FAMILY FOOTWEAR
Crochet and knit patterns by the staff of WORKBASKET Magazine

ISBN: 0-86675-305-2

TABLE OF CONTENTS

USEFUL INFORMATION

INTRODUCTION

It is hard to think of a more ideal project for the first-time knitter or crocheter than a pair of slippers. They are utilitarian, comfortable, and usually worn in the privacy of home where a mistake or two in the work is not even noticed. My very first "real" knitting project was a pair of slippers that I proudly completed long before I left grammar school.

Slipper patterns, though among the easiest of knitted or crocheted designs, are seldom boring. Accomplished knitters and crocheters will find countless ways to personalize a pattern, adding an embellishment or changing a color here or there to make a truly unique pair of slippers.

In this book we have compiled a collection of slippers for the entire family — from practical, utilitarian slippers to whimsical and fun footwear. Whether you're looking for a slipper-sock pattern for Dad, a cute pair of booties for baby, or perhaps even a crazy character slipper for a gag gift, this book has them all.

As an added bonus, each and every pattern in the book is presented in large, easy-to-read type. Whether you are a first-time knitter or crocheter or a veteran needleworker, we're certain your eyes will appreciate this particular feature.

Slippers make wonderful gifts and once you've given one pair, you're sure to get many requests for more. The patterns we have chosen for this book should keep your fingers happily busy, and your family's feet comfortably warm, for years to come.

Executive Editor
WORKBASKET Magazine

High Top Booties
(Knit)

page 92

Foot Cozies
(Knit)

page 89

Funny Bunny Footwear
(Knit)

page 64

Bedtime Buddy Slippers
(Crochet)

page 28

Lazy Days Slippers
(Crochet)

page 26

Sweet Dreams Slippers
(Crochet)

page 58

Cozy Cuddle Slippers
(Knit)

page 42

Mouse in the House Slippers
(Knit)

page 46

Papa's Pipe & Slippers
(Crochet)

page 51

Indian-Style Slippers
(Crochet)

page 61

Fringed Moccasins
(Crochet)

page 34

Harvest Time Slippers
(Knit)

page 44

Sofa Loafers
(Crochet)

page 54

Night Owl Slippers
(Knit)

page 38

Slam Dunk Slippers
(Crochet)

page 18

Bathtime Boots

(Crochet)

page 78

Pink Poodle Slippers

(Crochet)

page 82

Lounging Slippers

(Knit)

page 72

Slender Silhouette Slippers
(Crochet)

page 76

Raspberry Rhapsody Slippers
(Crochet)

page 31

Corn In The Morn Slippers
(Knit)

page 68

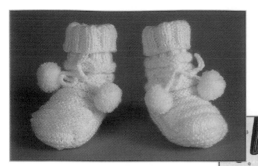

Graceful Baby Booties
(Knit)

page 24

Midnight Snack Attack Slipper-Socks
(Knit)

page 86

Family of Fish Slippers
(Knit)

page 12

ABBREVIATIONS AND TERMS

Crochet

bl	block stitch		**p**	picot
CC	Contrasting Color		**pc**	popcorn stitch
ch(s)	chain(s)		**rnd**	round
cl	cluster		**sc**	single crochet
dc	double crochet		**sk**	skip
dec	decrease		**sl st**	slip stitch
dtr	double treble crochet		**sp(s)**	space(s)
hdc	half double crochet		**st**	stitch
inc	increase		**tr**	treble crochet
lp	loop		**tr tr**	treble treble crochet
MC	Main Color		**yo**	yarn over

Knit

CC	Contrasting Color		**rnd**	round
dec	decrease		**sk**	skip
inc	increase		**sl**	slip
K	knit		**sp**	space
lp	loop		**st**	stitch
MC	Main Color		**tbl**	through back loop
P	purl		**tog**	together
psso	pass slip stitch over		**yo**	yarn over

Gauge — The number of stitches to the inch horizontally and the number of rows to the inch vertically.

Work Even — Continue working the pattern without increasing or decreasing the row length by adding or omitting any stitches.

GONE FISHING

Family of Fish
SLIPPERS

*These funny fish slippers are designed with
real anglers in mind: there are three sizes
each for minnows, keepers and even lunkers.*

I sn't this the limit? A special purl stitch gives these slippers a real fish scale texture. They look so realistic that even the game warden may think something's fishy. There's a size to fit everyone in the entire family with this pattern so knit up a mess of 'em.

Directions are given for a child's size (called "min-nows"); youth sizes (called "keepers") and adult sizes (called "lunkers") follow in parentheses.

Materials: About 325 (650,650) yards worsted weight yarn in a fish-like color, small amount of similar yarn of a contrasting color such as gray or silver, number 9 knitting needles, a tapestry needle and four "eye" buttons (work French knots for eyes in slippers intended for children younger than three years of age). If using animal eye type buttons as shown in photograph, you'll also need a pair of garden pruning shears and a small amount of foam padding or felt.

Finished Measurements:

Minnows — Width is 2-1/2 inches; length minus tail is approximately 4 inches (small), 5 inches (medium) and 6 inches (large).

Keepers — Width is 3 inches; length minus tail approximately 7 inches (small), 8 inches (medium) and 9 inches (large).

Lunkers — Width is 3-1/4 inches; length minus tail is approximately 10 inches (small), 11 inches (medium) and 12 inches (large).

Gauge: Working in garter stitch on number 9 needles with double strand of yarn, 4 stitches and 7 rows equal 1 inch.

TO SAVE TIME, TAKE TIME TO CHECK GAUGE.

With double strand of yarn, cast on 23(29,35) sts.

ROW 1 P1, *sl one as to P, P1, repeat from * two (three, four) times, K9 (11,13), P1, *sl one as to P, P1, repeat from * two (three, four) times. **ROWS 2 and 4** P8(10,12), K7(9,11), P8(10,12). **ROW 3** P2, *sl one as to P, P1, repeat from * one (two, three) time(s), P1, K9(11,13), P2, *sl one as to P, P1, repeat from * one (two, three) time(s), P1. Repeat Rows 1-4 until 1-1/2 (2, 2-1/2 inches) from desired length, ending

with an even row.

Toe Shaping: (For Minnows: Skip to Row 5.) **ROW 1** K. **ROW 2 and all even rows** P. (For Keepers: Go to Row 3. For Lunkers: Repeat Rows 1 and 2. **Next Row:** *K5, K2 tog, repeat from * across — 30 sts. **Next Row:** P.) **ROW 3** *K4, K2 tog, repeat from * across (For Keepers only: End row with K5.) — 25 sts. **ROW 5** *K3, K2 tog, repeat from * across. (For Minnows Only: End with K3 — 19 sts; for Keepers and Lunkers — 20 sts.) **ROW 7** *K2, K2 tog, repeat from * across. (For Minnows Only: End with

K3.) — 15 sts. **ROW 9** *K1, K2 tog, repeat from * across — 10 sts. Measure approximately 2 feet of yarn, cut. With tapestry needle draw up remaining stitches and fasten securely. Sew up top seam leaving adequate opening for foot.

Tail Fin: (Make four — two for each slipper.) With CC, cast on 11(13,15) sts. **ROW 1** *K2, pick up lp between needles and place it on the left needle then K this lp through the back

(called inc 1), K2(3,4), sl one P-wise, K2 tog, psso, K2(3,4), inc 1, K2. **ROWS 2, 4, 6, 8, 10 and 12** P. **ROW 3** Drop CC, join MC, repeat Row 1. **ROW 5** K. **ROWS 7,9 and 11** K2 tog, K to within last 2 sts, K2 tog. Bind off.

Top and Side Fins: (Make 6). With either MC or CC, cast on 2(4,4) sts. **ROWS 1, 3 and 5** K1, P1 across. **ROWS 2 and 4** K1, P1 across, ending by casting on 2 sts. Bind off in ribbing.

Finishing: With wrong sides together, sew tail fins together. Sew up back seam of slippers and sew tail fins in place over seam. Sew side fins in place near beginning of toe shaping. Attach buttons in place for eyes. Sew top fin in place over seam.

Note: Animal eyes as shown in photograph are attached with a metal ring that clamps into a shank. The protruding shank may make the slippers uncomfortable to wear. If using shank type eyes, trim the shank after securing it in place. Ordinary garden pruning shears work well. Sew a patch of foam padding (available in craft stores) or felt over the trimmed shanks on the inside of the slipper. This patch is not necessary if you are using regular buttons. Regular flat buttons can be sewn in place and wiggle eyes can be glued over them, if desired. Slippers intended for children younger than 3 years old should not contain buttons. Instead, make French knots with a contrasting color yarn for eyes.

SLAM DUNK SLIPPERS

These high-top slippers are cute as well as practical. What's more, they're child-tested and mother-approved!

Designed by a mother of several little ones, these mock athletic shoe baby slippers are sized to fit right. Because they use regular shoe laces instead of satin ribbon for ties, these slippers won't work their way off an active toddler's feet.

Sizes are given corresponding to actual shoes size. Directions are for size 1 with changes for size 2, 3 and 4 in parentheses.

Materials: About 180 yard red, white and blue sport weight yarn; a size F crochet hook; and a pair of 18-inch shoe laces.

Finished Measurements:
Length of Sole: 3-1/2 (4, 4-1/2, 5) inches

Shown in color on page 7

Width of Sole: 2 (2, 2-1/2, 2-1/2) inches

Height at Back of Ankle: 2-3/4 (2-3/4, 3-1/2, 3-1/2) inches

Gauge: 5 sc and 5 rows equal 1 inch.

TO SAVE TIME, TAKE TIME TO CHECK GAUGE.

Note: Unless specified, always work sts through both lps of sc and dc. Sole is worked in rnds. Do not turn work at end of each rnd.

Sole: With blue, ch 11(13,14,16). **RND 1** 3 Sc in 2nd ch from hook, sc in each of next 8(10,11,13) ch sts, 3 sc in last ch. *Do not turn.* Continue sc in each of next 8(10,11,13) sts on opposite of ch, join with sl st to beginning of rnd — 22(26,28,32) sc. **RND 2** Ch 1, *2 sc in each of next 3 sc, sc in each of next 8(10, 11,13) sc, repeat from * once, join — 28(32,34,38) sc. **RND 3** Ch 1, *(2 sc in next sc, sc in next sc) three times, sc in each of next 8(10,11,13) sc, repeat from * once, join — 34(38,40,44) sc. **RND 4** Ch 1, *(2 sc in next sc, sc in each of next 2 sc) three times, sc in each of next 8(10,11,13) sc, repeat from * once, join — 40 (44,46,50) sc. **RND 5 — For Sizes 3 and 4 Only** Ch 1, *(2 sc in next sc, sc in each of next 3 sc) three times, sc in each of next 0(0,11,13) sc, repeat from * once, join — 0(0,52, 56) sc. **ALL SIZES** Sc in each sc around, join — 40(44,52,56) sc. Do not fasten off.

Lower Body of Foot: This part is worked in joined rows instead of rnds, so that the pattern will look the same when working ankle of slipper. Ch 3, turn. **ROW 1** With inside of sole facing you and working in front lps only, dc in 2nd sc from hook and in every sc around. Join white with sl st to top of ch-3 — 40(44,52,56) dc. Ch 1, turn. **ROW 2** With white, sc in every dc, ending with last sc worked in top of ch-3 — 40(44, 52,56) sc. Join blue. Ch 3, turn. **ROW 3** With blue, dc in 2nd sc from hook and in each sc, join — 40(44,52,56) dc. Fasten off. Mark the fourth (fourth, fifth, fifth) dc to left of joining.

Ankle: ROW 1 With outside of slipper facing you, join white yarn in marked st. Ch 1, sc in next 20(20,25,25) sc, beginning in st where

yarn is joined — 20(24, 27,31) sts remain for toe of slipper. Ch 3, turn. **ROW 2** Dc in 3rd sc from hook, dc in each of next 16(16,21,21) sc, sk 1 sc, dc in remaining sc — 18(18,23,23) dc. Ch 1, turn. **ROW 3** Sc in each of next 5(5,7,7) dc, sk 1 dc, sc in each of next 6(6,7,7) dc, sk 1 dc, sc in each of next 5(5,7,7) dc, ending with last sc worked in top of ch-3 — 16 (16,21,21) sc. Ch 3, turn. **ROW 4** Dc in 3rd sc from hook, dc in each of next 12(12,17,17) sc, sk 1 sc, dc in remaining sc — 14 (14,19,19) dc. **ROW 5** — **Sizes 3 and 4 Only** Ch 1, turn. Sc in each st across row, ending with last sc worked in top of ch-3 — 19 sc. **ROW 6** — **Sizes 3 and 4 Only** Ch 3, turn. Dc in 3rd sc from

21

hook, dc in each of next 15 dc, sk 1 sc, dc in remaining sc — 17 dc. **ALL SIZES** With inside of slipper facing you, work 7(7, 10,10) sc across slanted ankle edge, working 2 sc in each dc row and 1 sc in each sc row, ending with 1 sc in st where yarn was joined to crochet ankle. Fasten off. **Other Slanted Edge:** With inside of slipper facing you, join yarn in st where last st of Row 1 of ankle was worked. Ch 1, work 7(7,10,10) sc across slanted ankle edge, placing 1 sc in st where yarn was joined, and working 1 sc in each sc row and 2 sc in each dc row. Join with sl st to top ch-3 of last row of ankle. Fasten off.

Upper Toe and Tongue: With red, ch 14(16,18,20). **ROW 1** (Right Side) Beginning in 2nd ch from hook, sc in each of next 12(14, 16,18) ch, 3 sc in last ch. *Do not turn.* Continue sc in each of next 12(14, 16,18) sc on opposite side of ch — 27(31,35,39) sc. Ch 3, turn. **ROW 2** Beginning in 2nd sc from hook, dc in each of next 11(13,15,17) dc, 3 dc in each of next 3 sc, dc in each of the next 12(14,16,18) sc. Ch 1, turn. **ROW 3** Sc in each of the next 12(14, 16,18) dc, *2 sc in each of next 1(1,2,2) dc, sc in each of the next 2(2,1,1) dc, repeat from * twice, sc in each of next 10(12, 13,14) dc, working last sc in top of ch-3. Mark eighth (eighth, tenth, tenth) st from each corner on long sides of tongue. Work 6 sc along straight short edge of tongue, join with sl st to first sc of row. Fasten off.

Join upper toe and tongue to lower body of slipper as follows: Place pieces wrong sides together, matching upper toe portion of tongue and lower body of slipper. With outside of slipper facing you, join red at bottom of left slanted edge. Sc back lp of lower body and front lp part of upper toe between markers — 20 (24,27,31) sc.

Upper Edging and Eyelets: With red and starting at bottom of slanted edge, work 1(1,2, 2) hdc, *ch 1, sk 1 sc, 1 hdc, repeat from * two (two, three, three) times. Work 2 sc in top corner, sc across top of slipper, 2 sc in other top corner, 1 hdc in first sc of slanted edge, *ch 1, sk 1 sc, 1 hdc, repeat from * two (two, three, three) times, work 1(1,2,2) hdc, join with sl st to first sc worked when joining upper toe to lower body, turn.

Sl st in sts on slanted edge. Ch 1, turn. With outside of slipper facing you and working from left to right, work a row of reverse sc across top of ankle, turn. Sl st in sts along other slanted edge. Fasten off.

Sole Edging: With red and bottom of sole facing away from you, join yarn in the back lp of a sc in the heel portion of slipper. Ch 1, sc in the back lps around bottom of slipper, join with sl st. Fasten off.

Weave in ends. Make second slipper same as first. Thread laces through eyelets. Hand stitch purchased star-shaped appliqués, if desired.

23

Graceful Baby BOOTIES

Delicate stitches make these booties pretty enough for special occasions but practical enough for baby to wear most every day.

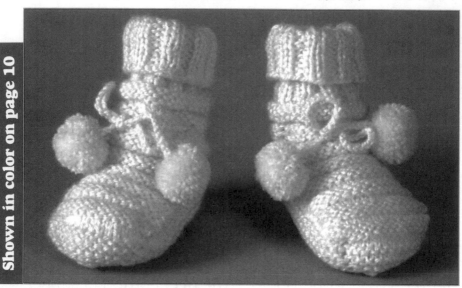

Shown in color on page 10

Some baby booties are made for show — they look nice but they don't stay put on tiny feet. These booties, however, stay snug and secure on even the most active little toes. They're pretty enough for a princess but they'll suit a little prince just as well.

Directions are given in a size that stretches and fits most infants.

Materials: About 300 yards baby or fingering weight yarn and number 2 knitting needles.

Finished Measurements: The sole measures approximately 2 x 3-1/2 inches.

Gauge: 6 sts equal 1 inch.

TO SAVE TIME, TAKE TIME TO CHECK GAUGE.

Cast on 42 sts. **ROW 1** Sl 1, K across. **ROW 2** Sl 1, yo, K20, yo, K20, yo, K1. **ROWS 3, 5, 7, 9, 11, 13 and 15** Sl 1, K across. **ROW 4** Sl 1, yo, K21, yo, K1, yo, K21, yo, K1. **ROW 6** Sl 1, K22, yo, K3, yo, K23. **ROW 8** Sl 1, K22, yo, K5, yo, K23. **ROW 10** Sl 1, K22, yo, K7, yo, K23. **ROW 12** Sl 1, K22, yo, K9, yo, K23. **ROW 14** Sl 1, K22, yo, K11, yo, K23. **ROW 16** Sl 1, K22, yo, K13, yo, K23 — 61 sts. **ROW 17** Sl 1, P across. **ROW 18** Sl 1, K36, K next 2 tog, turn. **ROW 19** Sl 1, K13, K next 2 tog, turn.

ROW 20 Sl 1, P13, P next 2 tog, turn. **ROW 21** Sl 1, K13, K next 2 tog, turn.

Repeat Rows 19, 20 and 21 six more times. Repeat Row 19. Repeat Row 20 — 37 sts.

NEXT ROW — ROW 42 Sl 1, K across. **ROW 43** Sl 1, K across. **ROW 44** Sl 1, P across. **ROW 45** Sl 1, K across. Repeat Rows 43, 44 and 45 three more times. **NEXT ROW — ROW 55** K1, *yo, K2 tog, K1*, repeat between *'s. **ROW 56** Sl 1, P across. **ROW 57** Sl 1, K across. Repeat Rows 43, 44 and 45 three more times.

Work in K2, P2 ribbing for 2 inches. Bind off loosely. Sew back and sole seams. Crochet a 12-inch chain for tie. Weave tie through spaces at ankle and make pom-poms for ends of ties.

Lazy Days
SLIPPERS

Some days are meant for lounging, and a pair of soft, comfortable slippers is perfect for the times you want to wear a robe all day and be lazy.

Soft, stretchy and topped off with a big floppy pom-pom, these slippers will suit you well whenever relaxation is what you seek. Prop up a few pillows, take out a good book or have the television remote handy and these lazy days slippers will keep you company. Don't have time to relax? Well, at least let your feet enjoy themselves.

Directions are given for women's size small, with changes for sizes medium and large in parentheses.

Materials: About 325 yards worsted weight yarn, a size G crochet hook and a tapestry needle.

Finished Measurements:
Small: 7 inches long
Medium: 8 inches long
Large: 9 inches long

Gauge: 4 sts equal 1 inch; 4 rows equal 1 inch.

TO SAVE TIME, TAKE TIME TO CHECK GAUGE.

Ch 42. **ROW 1** Sc in 2nd ch from hook, and in next 20 sts, 3 sc in next st, mark for center st, sc in next 20 sts. Ch 1, turn. **ROW 2** Sc in each of next 20 sts, 3 sc in next st, sc in next 21 sts. Ch 1, turn.

Repeat Row 2 for

Shown in color on page 4

9(11,13) rows, finding one st added on both sides of center mark and 3 sc in center mark of each row. Piece will look like a big V.

NEXT ROW Sc in each st — 59 (63, 67) sts. Ch 1, turn. Work this row three more times. Fasten off leaving about 30 inches of yarn. Sew bottom and back. Turn right side out. Attach pom-pom or ribbon with matching or desired color.

Pom-pom: Wind 20 strands of yarn around a 1-inch (or any size you wish) cardboard, tie around center, cut ends and trim into a ball.

Bedtime Buddy
SLIPPERS

Loopy stitches covering the out-side of these slippers make them almost as "furry" as a stuffed animal and a perfect buddy for a child at bedtime.

A ny little child would love having these soft, furry-looking slippers part of the bedtime scene. From pajama time, right through the bedtime snack, nighttime story and last-minute drink of water, these slippers will be part of the evening ritual for the lucky youngster who owns a pair.

Shown in color on page 4

Directions are given for child's size small with changes for medium and large sizes in parentheses.

Materials: About 350 yards worsted weight yarn, a tapestry needle and a size H crochet hook.

Finished Measurements: 5(6,7) inches long

Gauge: 3 lp sts equal 1 inch.

TO SAVE TIME, TAKE TIME TO CHECK GAUGE.

Special Abbreviations: Double Lp St — insert hook in st, winding yarn clockwise, wind yarn twice around index finger, insert hook from left to right through lps on finger, pick up both lps and pull through st, drop lps from finger, yarn over and pull through all lps on hook.

Slipper: Ch 21(23,25). **ROW 1** Sc in 2nd st from hook and in each remaining st of ch. Ch 1 to turn on all rows. **ROW 2** Work 1 double lp st in each st. **ROW 3** Sc in each st. **ROWS 4, 5, 6 and 7** Repeat Rows 2 and 3 twice. **ROWS 8-13** Work in sc for sole. **ROWS 14, 16 and 18** Work in double lp st. **ROWS 15 and 17** Work in sc. Fasten off.

Finishing: Fold slipper in half, match rows of one side and sew seam. Sew first and last rows of slipper together for about 4 inches from seam. Sew other side edge together, matching rows, for back seam.

Raspberry Rhapsody
SLIPPERS

Relive memories with the lyrics to the old song:
"When I was young my slippers were red;
I could kick up my heels right over my head..."

Shown in color on page 9

These pretty slippers can be made with any color yarn, but they're especially pretty in red. The stitches resemble the delicate texture of raspberries. Make some for Christmas or Valentine's Day. A bowl of raspberries is optional, but delicious!

31

Directions are given for women's size small, medium and large.

Materials: About 325 yards worsted weight yarn and a size H crochet hook.

Finished Measurements:
Small: 8-1/2 inches long
Medium: 9-1/2 inches long
Large: 10-1/2 inches long

Gauge: 4 sts equal 1 inch; 4 rows equal 1 inch.

TO SAVE TIME, TAKE TIME TO CHECK GAUGE.

Cuff: Starting at top, ch 83. **ROW 1** Sc in 2nd ch from hook, *sk next 2 ch, sc in next ch, repeat from * across — 28 sc. Ch 1, turn. **ROWS 2-7** Sc in each sc across. Ch 1, turn.

Heel: (First Half) **ROW 1** Sc in first 7 sc. Ch 1, turn. **ROWS 2-9** Working over these 7 sts only, sc in each sc across. Ch 1, turn.

To Turn Heel: (Center Edge) **ROW 1** Dec one sc at beginning of row. Dec by inserting hook in next st, yo and draw up a lp, insert hook in next st, yo and draw up a lp, yo and draw though all 3 lps (dec made). Sc across. Ch 1, turn. **ROW 2** Sc across to last 2 sc, dec 1 sc. **ROW 3** Repeat Row 1. **ROW 4** Repeat Row 2 — 3 sts remain. Fasten off.

Heel: (Second Half) Sk the 14 center sts on last row of cuff, join yarn in next st, sc in joining and in last 6 sc — 7 sc total. Ch 1, turn. Continue to work as for first half of heel, reversing shaping. (The decs are at center edge.) Fasten off.

Join yarn to first st at side edge of last row on

first half, sc in joining and next 2 sc, make 11 sc along center edge of heel, placing a marker in next st, sc in next 14 sc, place a marker in last st just made, make 11 sc along center edge, then sc in 3 sc of last row of second half — 42 sc. Ch 1, turn.

Note: Move markers up into st directly above marked st after each row has been completed.

Instep: ROW 1 Sc in each sc to within 2 sts before marked st, dec 1 sc, sc in each sc to next marked st, dec 1 sc, sc to end of row. Ch 1, turn. **ROW 2** Sc in each sc across. Repeat Rows 1 and 2 of instep alternately until 28 sts remain, removing markers on last row. Work even until total length, from center of heel, is 6-1/2 inches for small size, 7-1/2 inches for medium size and 8-1/2 inches for large size (2 inches less than desired finished length).

Toe: ROW 1 Sc in first 5 sts, (dec 1 sc) twice, sc in next 10 sc, (dec 1 sc) twice, sc in last 5 sc. Ch 1, turn. **ROW 2** Sc in each sc across. Ch 1, turn. **ROW 3** Sc in first 4 sc, (dec 1 sc) twice, sc in next 8 sc, (dec 1 sc) twice, sc in last 4 sc. Ch 1, turn. **ROW 4** Repeat Row 2.

Continue in this manner, dec 4 sts on every other row, making decs over decs, until 8 sts remain. Fasten off. Sew seam and toe. Press lightly.

Make second slipper the same way.

FRINGED MOCCASINS

*Beads and fringe embellish these sturdy
moccasin slippers that closely resemble the real thing.
You'll love wearing them around the tepee.*

Shown in color on page 6

34

Cool, crisp fall evenings won't leave you with cold feet when you're wearing a pair of these fringed moccasins. They're realistic enough to wear with a costume for Halloween — but save them for indoor festivities.

Directions are given for size small with medium and large in parentheses.

Materials: About 650 yards worsted weight rust colored yarn, a size G crochet hook, 12 turquoise pony beads, two white pony beads, a small amount of gold worsted weight yarn, safety pins to use as stitch markers and a tapestry needle.

Finished Measurements:
Small: 7-1/2 inches in length
Medium: 9-1/2 inches in length
Large: 12 inches in length

Gauge: 17 sc equal 4 inches.

TO SAVE TIME, TAKE TIME TO CHECK GAUGE.

Note: Mark the first st of each round with a safety pin.

Sole: With two strands of yarn, ch 22(26,34). **RND 1** 2 Sc in 2nd ch from hook, sc in next 19(23,31) ch, 5 hdc in last ch, working along back side of ch, sc in next 19(23,31) ch, 2 sc in last ch — 47 (55,71) sts. **RND 2** 2 Sc in next 2 sts, sc in next 19(23,31) sts, 2 sc in next 5 sts, sc in next 19(23,31) sts, 2 sc in next st, sc in remaining st — 55(63,79) sts. **RND 3** *Sc in next st, 2 sc in next st*, repeat between *'s, sc in next 19(23,31) sts, repeat between *'s five times, sc in next 20(24,32) sts, 2 sc in next st, sc in remaining st — 63(71,87) sts. **RND 4** *2 Sc in next st, sc in next 2 sts*, repeat between *'s, sc in next 18(22,30) sts, repeat between *'s six times, sc in next 18(22,30) sts, 2 sc in next st, sc in remaining 2 sts — 72(80,96) sts. **RND 5** *2 Sc in next st, sc in next 3 sts*, repeat between *'s, sc in next 18(20,28) sts, repeat between *'s six (seven, seven) times, sc in next 18(20,28) sts, 2 sc in next st, sc in remaining 3 sts — 81 (90,106) sts. **RND 6** 2 Sc in next st, sc in next 4 sts, repeat between *'s, sc in next 18(20,28) sts, repeat between *'s six (seven, seven) times, sc in next 18(20,28) sts, 2 sc in next st, sc in remaining 4 sts — 90(100,116) sts. **RND 7** Sc in next st and each st around. **RND 8** Working in back lps only, sl st in next st and each st around.

Upper: Work two (three, three) rnds of hdc. **RND 1** Sc in next 2(3,3) sts, (dec over next 2 sts) twice, sc in next 33 (39,47) sts, (dec over next 2 sts, sc in next st) six times, sc in next 31 (34,42) sc, dec over remaining 2 sts — 81 (91,107) sts. **RND 2** Sc in next 6(8,8) sts, dec over next 2 sts, sc in next 27(32,39) sts, (dec over next 2 sts, sc in next st) six times, sc in next 26 (29,38) sc, dec over remaining 2 sts — 73 (83,99) sts. **RND 3** Sc in next 31(38,45) sts, (dec over next 2 sts, sc in next st) six times, sc in next 24(27,36) sts — 67(77, 93) sts. **RND 4** Sc in next

34(40,47) sc, dec over next 2 sts, sc in next 3 sts, dec over next 2 sts, sc in next 26(30,39) sts — 65(75,91) sts. **RND 5** In this round, you'll be working the top portion of the slipper and joining it to the sides by working a portion in rows. Sc in next 33(39,46) sc. *Dec over next 2 sts, place marker, sc in next 3 sts, dec over next 2 sts, sl st in next st, turn. Repeat from * 10(13,15) times. Continue sc around to end-of-rnd marker. **RNDS 6 and 7 — For Medium and Large Sizes Only** Sc to 2 sts before center top marker, dec over next 2 sts, sc in next 3 sts, dec over next 2 sts, sc to end-of-rnd marker. **RNDS 8 and 9 — For Size Large Only** Repeat Rnds 6 and 7. **NEXT RND — All**

Sizes Join with a sl st — 45(45,53) sts.

Cuff: RND 1 Ch 1, sc in next st and each st around, join with sl st. **RND 2** Ch 3, dc in next st and each st around, join with sl st to top of ch. **RND 3** Ch 2, hdc in next st and each st around, join with sl st to top of ch. Fasten off.

Finishing: Referring to photo for placement, sew beads to top of slipper and cross stitch with gold yarn.

Lace Ties: With rust yarn and a single strand, ch for about 20 inches or desired length. Lace the tie in between the dc posts on the cuff.

Fringe: With rust, cut 4-inch lengths and attach fringe to the edge of cuff. Trim to even ends, if necessary.

Night Owl
SLIPPERS

Three simple cable rows and two tiny buttons create owls on these slippers especially appropriate for folks who come alive when the sun goes down.

These slippers are made in three pieces: a double sole, a back and a front. The owl design is created with three simple rows of easy cable stitches.

Directions are given for size small with any changes for sizes medium and large in parentheses.

Materials: About 500 yards wool blend knitting worsted weight yarn in main color (MC) and a contrasting color (CC), number 8 knitting needles, cable needle, a tapestry needle, four small white buttons, sewing needle and thread and a size G crochet hook.

Finished Measurements: Length: 8(9,10) inches

Width: Each size measures 3-1/2 inches wide (slipper will stretch to comfortably conform with most average-size feet).

Gauge: With number 8 knitting needles and double strand of yarn, 4 sts and 6 rows equal 1 inch. **TO SAVE TIME, TAKE TIME TO CHECK GAUGE.**

Special Abbreviations:

Shown in color on page 7

(C4B) Cable Four Back — Work on 4 sts. Place first 2 sts on cable needle, hold in back of work, K2, then K2 from cable needle.

(C4F) Cable Four Front — Work on 4 sts. Place first 2 sts on cable needle, hold in front of work, K2, then K2 from cable needle.

Note: All work is done with a double strand of yarn.

Sole: (Make one of MC and one of color CC). Cast on 6 sts. **ROW 1 and All Odd Rows** P across. **ROW 2** Inc 1 in first st, K to within last st, inc 1 — 8 sts. **ROW 4** Repeat Row 2 — 10 sts. **ROW 6** Repeat Row 2 — 12 sts. **ROW 8** K across. Repeat Rows 8 and 9 six (eight, 10) times. **ROW 10** Repeat Row 2 — 14 sts. **ROW 12** Repeat Row 2 — 16 sts. **ROW 14** K across. Repeat Rows 14 and 15 two (three, four) times. **ROW 16** Sl 1, K1, psso, K to within last 2 sts, K2 tog — 14 sts. **ROWS 18 and 20** K across. **ROW 22** Repeat Row 16 — 12 sts. **ROW 24** Repeat Row 16 — 10 sts. **ROW 26** Repeat Row 16 — 8 sts. **ROW 28** Repeat Row 16 — 6 sts. **ROW 29** P across. Bind off.

Finishing: Position wrong sides of soles (MC and CC) together. Use crochet hook and two strands of MC yarn to join soles with sc around entire edge of sole. Set aside.

Front: (Make one.) With CC, beginning at toe edge, cast on 10 sts. **ROW 1 and All Odd Rows Except Where Otherwise Noted** P across. **ROW 2** Inc 1 in first st, K to within last st, inc 1 — 12 sts. **ROW 4** Repeat Row 2 — 14 sts. **ROW 6** Repeat Row 2 — 16 sts. **ROW 8** Repeat Row 2 — 18 sts. **ROW 10** Repeat Row 2 — 20 sts. **ROW 12** Repeat Row 2 — 22 sts. **ROW 14** Repeat Row 2 — 24 sts. **ROW 15** P5, K14, P5. **ROW 16** Repeat Row 2 — 26 sts. **ROW 17** P6, K14, P6. **ROW 18** Inc 1 in first st, K6, P2, C4B, C4F, P2, K6, inc 1 in last st — 28 sts. **ROW 19** P7, K3, P8, K3, P7. **ROW 20** Inc 1 in first st, K7, P2, K8, P2, K7, inc 1 in last st — 30 sts. **ROW 21** P8, K3, P8, K3, P8.

ROW 22 Inc 1 in first st, K8, P2, K8, P2, K8, inc 1 in last st — 32 sts. ROW 23 P9, K3, P8, K3, P9. ROW 24 Inc 1 in first st, K9, P2, K8, P2, K9, inc 1 in last st — 34 sts. ROW 25 P10, K3, P8, K3, P10. ROW 26 Inc 1 in first st, K10, P2, C4B, C4F, P2, K10, inc 1 in last st — 36 sts. ROW 27 P11, K3, P8, K3, P11. ROW 28 Inc 1 in first st, K11, P2, K8, P2, K11, inc 1 in last st — 38 sts. ROW 29 P12, K3, P8, K3, P12. ROW 30 Inc 1 in first st, K12, P2, C4B, C4F, P2, K12, inc 1 in last st — 40 sts. ROW 31 P14, K12, P14. ROWS 32, 34 and 36 Inc 1 in first st, K to last st, inc 1— 46 sts at end of Row 36. ROW 33 P15, K12, P15. ROWS 35 and 37 P. ROW 38 Drop CC, join MC and K across. ROW 39 *K1, P1, repeat from * across. ROWS 40-42 Repeat Row 39. Bind off in ribbing.

Finishing: With sewing needle and thread, sew buttons in place for eyes.

Back: With MC, cast on 3 sts. ROW 1 Inc 1 in first st, P1, inc 1 in last st — 5 sts. ROW 2 Inc 1 in first st, *P1, K1, repeat from * to within last st, inc 1 — 7 sts. Repeat Row 2 until there are 45 sts on needle. Bind off in ribbing.

Finishing: Sew bottom edge of back to back of sole. Beginning at toe, sew front of slipper to front of sole, around side of sole, overlapping with back section (overlap will vary according to size). Start at toe and repeat along slipper's other side.

Make second slipper the same as the first.

Cozy Cuddle
SLIPPERS

*Super simple to make, these slippers should be
the ones you try even if you've never knit
another thing before in your life!*

The little cuffs on these knit slippers
are formed by only two purl stitches
every other row. They're surprisingly
comfortable and will fold down flat for

packing in your suitcase — you won't want to be without them, even for a single night.

One-size-fits-most for these easy-to-make wo-men's slippers.

Materials: About 325 yards worsted weight yarn, number 6 standard knitting needles and a tapestry needle. Add a simple crocheted edging and pom-pom in a contrasting color, if desired.

Finished Measurements: These stretchy, pliable slippers will fit most any woman's feet.

Gauge: 5 sts equal 1 inch; 8 rows equal 1 inch.

TO SAVE TIME, TAKE TIME TO CHECK GAUGE.

Cast on 52 sts. **ROW 1** K. **ROW 2** K7, P1, K36, P1, K7. Repeat Rows 1 and 2 until you have 20 ridges (40 rows). Bind off 8 sts beginning of next 2 rows — 36 sts. Continue in pattern until you have a total of 30 ridges (60 rows). **ROW 61** *K2, K2 tog, repeat from * to end of row — 27 sts. **ROWS 62-64** K. **ROW 65** *K1, K2 tog, repeat from * to end of row — 18 sts. **ROWS 66-68** K. **ROW 69** *K2 tog, repeat from * to end of row — 9 sts. **ROW 70** K.

Fasten off, leaving an 18-inch length of yarn. Draw yarn through sts on needle, gather, and use remaining length to sew top of slipper together. Sew back seam.

If desired, crochet edging in same or contrasting color and add pom-poms.

Harvest Time
SLIPPERS

Big chunky stitches made with four strands
of yarn form the pattern for these extra warm,
cuddly boots that will keep the frost off your toes.

I f you've ever needed a pattern for a quick pair of slippers, look no further. With extra large knitting needles and using four strands of yarn, these slippers will be finished in no time. The big, chunky pattern stitch will remind you of colorful Indian corn, especially if you choose yarn in autumn colors.

Directions are given for size small with size medium and size large in parentheses.

Materials: About 650 yards worsted weight yarn in two different colors, a tapestry needle and number 15 standard knitting needles.

Finished Measurements:
Small: 8 inches long
Medium: 9 inches long
Large: 10 inches long

Gauge: 5 sts equal 2 inches, 3 rows equal 1 inch.

TO SAVE TIME, TAKE TIME TO CHECK GAUGE.

Using four strands of yarn (two of each color), cast on 26(29,32) sts.

Pattern Stitch: ROW 1 P. **ROW 2** P10(11,12), K1, P4(5,6) K1, P10 (11,12).

Repeat Rows 1 and 2 until 11(13,15) rows have been completed, ending with Row 1. There will be 5(6,7) ridges on right side of slipper. Working in Pattern Stitch, bind off 6 sts at beginning of each of next 2 rows—14(17,20) sts.

Work even in pattern st for 8(12,16) more rows — 10(12,14) ridges on right side of work. **NEXT ROW** Dec 3 sts (P2 tog in each third of slipper) — 11(14,17) sts.

Continue to work in pattern for 6 more rows.

NEXT ROW (Dec Row) P2 tog across row. **NEXT ROW** P. Fasten off.

Draw ends of yarn through remaining sts on needle. Pull tog and fasten. Using same yarn, sew top and front of slipper, then sew back slipper seam. Take care to match rows and sts. Weave in yarn ends.

Mouse in the House SLIPPERS

Kitty-cats will be confused when the entire family is wearing mice on their feet. These fun, novelty slippers are sized for everyone!

Shown in color on page 5

You won't mind mice in your house when a pair of them are keeping each family member's feet warm and safe from winter drafts. These slippers are easy to make and are sized for feet from tiny tots to men's large.

Directions are given in child's size small (youth and adult size small follow in parentheses). For larger sizes than those given, work even until 2-1/2 inches from desired length before starting the toe shaping.

Materials: 4-ply 100% acrylic worsted weight gray yarn (one to three 3-ounce skeins depending on size of slipper), number 9 knitting needles, two "eye" buttons, one black button, black thread and a size C crochet hook.

Finished Measurements: For child's sizes, width measures 2-1/2 inches with length of 5 inches (small); 5-1/2 inches (medium); and 6-inches (large). For youth sizes, width measures 3 inches with length of 7 inches (small); 7-1/2 inches (medium); and 8 inches (large.) For adult sizes, width measures 3-1/2 with length of 9 inches (small); 10 inches (medium) and 11 inches (large).

Gauge: Working garter stitch with two strands of yarn on number 9 needles, 4 sts and 7 rows equal 1 inch.

TO SAVE TIME, TAKE TIME TO CHECK GAUGE.

With double strands of yarn, cast on 23(29,35) sts.

ROW 1 *K7(9,11), P1, K7(9,11), P1, K7(9,11). **ROW 2** K across. Repeat these two rows until piece measures 1-1/2 (2,2-1/2) inches less than the desired length, ending with a Row 1.

Toe Shaping:

(Child sizes) **ROWS 1, 3 and 5** *P1, K1, repeat from * across. **ROWS 2 and 4** *K1, P1, repeat from * across. **ROW 6** P2 tog across, ending with P1 — 12 sts. **ROW 7** K2 tog across — 6 sts. **ROW 8** P2 tog across — 3 sts. Cut yarn, leaving about 12 inches. With a tapestry needle, draw the yarn through remaining sts.

(Youth sizes) **ROWS 1, 3, 5 and 7** P1, *K1, P1, repeat from * across. **ROWS 2, 4, 6 and 8** K1, *P1, K1, repeat from * across. **ROW 9** K1, *K2

tog, repeat from * across — 15 sts. **ROW 10** P1, *P2 tog, repeat from * across — 8 sts. **ROW 11** K2 tog across — 4 sts. Cut yarn, leaving about 14 inches. With tapestry needle, draw yarn through remaining sts.

(Adult sizes) **ROWS 1, 3, 5, 7, 9 and 11** P1, *K1, P1, repeat from * across. **ROWS 2, 4, 6, 8, 10 and 12** K1, *P1, K1, repeat from * across. **ROW 13** K1, *K2 tog, repeat from * across — 18 sts. **ROW 14** P2 tog across — 9 sts. **ROW 15** K1, *K2 tog, repeat from * across — 5 sts. Cut yarn, leaving about 16 inches of yarn. With tapestry needle, draw yarn through remaining sts.

Ears: (Make two for each slipper.) Work with a single strand of yarn.

(Child sizes) Cast on 6 sts. **ROWS 1 and 4** K. **ROW** 2 K4, turn, K4. **ROW** 3 K2, turn, K2. Repeat Rows 1-4 three times. Bind off.

(Youth sizes) Cast on 8 sts. **ROWS 1 and 5** K. **ROW** 2 K6, turn, K6. **ROW** 3 K4, turn, K4. **ROW** 4 K2, turn, K2. Repeat Rows 1-5 four times. Bind off.

(Adult sizes) Cast on 10 sts. **ROWS 1 and 6** K. **ROW** 2 K8, turn, K8. **ROW** 3 K6, turn, K6. **ROW** 4 K4, turn, K4. **ROW** 5 K2, turn, K2. Repeat Rows 1-6 five times. Bind off.

Whiskers and Nose: Cut six 3-inch lengths of black thread. Draw through tip of slipper, knot in center and trim to even. Sew round black button over knot to form nose. For slippers intended for children under the age of three, substitute a French knot of contrasting color in place of the button nose.

Finishing: Sew back and top seams, leaving opening for foot. Sew ears in place by first sewing cast on edge to bound off edge. Next sew two ears to the top of slipper, referring to photo for placement. Sew buttons in place for eyes; make eyes of French knots with contrasting color yarn for slippers intended for children under the age of three. With size C crochet hook, chain 15 to form tail and sew in place at back of slipper. Make second slipper the same.

Papa's Pipe &
SLIPPERS

*He'll have to supply the pipe, but if you give
him a pair of these traditional-looking slippers,
he'll feel like the king of his castle.*

Shown in color on page 5

Slippers with a built-in sock will keep Dad's (or Grandpa's) feet warm and relaxed as he sips his coffee, puffs his pipe and reads his favorite magazine. An ideal gift for Father's Day, or any other time you want to make the man in your life feel extra special.

Directions are given for a 10-inch long pair of slippers. To make larger or smaller slippers, change your hook size accordingly.

Materials:
About 325 yards main color (MC) and contrasting color (CC) worsted weight yarn, a tapestry needle, a size I crochet hook for the body of the slippers and a size G crochet hook for the cuff. To enlarge or reduce the pattern, change hook size accordingly. Sizes H and F are recommended for smaller slippers.

Finished Measurements: 10 inches long

Gauge: 7 hdc equal 2 inches; 5 rows equal 2 inches.

TO SAVE TIME, TAKE TIME TO CHECK GAUGE.

Sole: With larger hook and MC, ch 25. **RND 1** 4 Hdc in 3rd ch from hook, hdc in next 21 ch, 7 hdc in end ch (toe), 21 hdc along opposite side, join with sl st in top of beginning ch-3. **RND 2** Ch 2, hdc around, inc 4 sts at heel and 6 sts at toe. **RND 3** Ch 2, hdc around, inc 3 sts at heel and 5 sts at toe. **RND 4** Ch 2, hdc in each st around (no inc). **RND 5** Ch 1, sc in each st around. Fasten off.

Cuff: With MC and smaller hook, ch 22. **ROW 1** Sc in 2nd ch from hook and in each ch across — 21 sc. **ROWS 2-33** Ch 1, turn. Working in back lps only, sc in each sc across.

Cut yarn, leaving length long enough to sew up seam to make cuff. Fasten off.

Top of Foot: With larger hook, join CC to end of one cuff's ribs, ch 15. **RND 1** 5 Hdc in 3rd ch from hook, hdc in next 12 ch, 33 hdc around bottom of cuff, 12 hdc along opposite side of beginning ch, join with sl st in top of turning ch. **RND 2** Ch 2, hdc around, inc 5 sts at toe. **RND 3** Ch 2, hdc around, inc 4 sts at toe. **RNDS 4, 5 and 6** Hdc around (no inc), fasten off. **RND 7** With MC, work sc. Fasten off.

With MC sew top to sole. Turn down cuff, if desired.

SOFA LOAFERS

*For the couch potato or armchair quarterback
in your life, these slippers should be ideal. They're
made to look like loafers, which suits their purpose.*

Do you sometimes think the man in your life and the sofa in your livingroom are permanently attached to one another? These slippers should suit the casual man quite well — they look nice and are designed for sofa loafing.

Directions are given for a man's one-size-fits-most slipper.

Materials: About 350 yards worsted weight yarn in main color (MC) and contrasting color (CC) and a size G crochet hook.

Finished Measurements:
Length: 11 inches
Width: 3-1/2 inches
Gauge: 4 sts equal 1 inch.
TO SAVE TIME, TAKE TIME TO CHECK GAUGE.
Sole: With MC, ch 40. **RND 1** Work 3 dc in 3rd st from hook, dc in each of next 2 sts, hdc in next 3 sts, sc in next 11 sts, hdc in next 4 sts, dc in next 13 sts, 2 dc in next st, hdc in next st, 5 sc in end st. Now work

in back side of ch: 2 dc in next st, dc in next 13 sts, hdc in next 4 sts, sc in next 11 sts, hdc in next 3 sts, dc in next 2 sts, 3 dc in next st (base of shell), sl st in top of first st. **RND 2** (2 sc in next st) three times, work 1 sc in each st around with 3 inc around toe with 2 sc between each inc, make 2 inc at end of row. **RND 3** Make an inc in next (center end) st, sc in next 2 sc, inc in next st, sc in next 18 sts, hdc in next 19 sts, 5 inc around toe with 1 hdc between increases, hdc in next 19 sts, sc in next 18 sts, inc in next st and inc at center end. **RND 4** (Sc in next 2 sc, 2 sc in next st) twice, work sc around with 5 incs around toe, making 2 sc between increases. Make 2 inc on side of heel. **RND 5** Sc in each st around. Fasten off.

Make a second sole using CC, then work together with pieces back-to-back, working one row of sc in CC.

Top: RND 1 With edge of sole toward you, sc in CC in center sl st at heel end of top sole, going through only the inside lp of sl st and working around in inside lps, dec one st over next two sts, sc in next st, dec over next two sts, sc in next 10 sts, dec over next 2 sts. Continue around with 4 dec around toe with 2 sc between decs. Make a dec across from heel then work to within last 6 sts, dec over next 2 sts, sc in next st, dec over next 2 sts, sl st in remaining st. **RND 2** Ch 1, turn. Sc in sl st, sc in each st around, sl st in first sc. Fasten off.

RND 3 Turn. In MC, sc in sl st, * make a long sc over next st by inserting hook down between Rows 1 and 2, sl one sc over next sc, inserting hook down between Rows 1 and 2, sc in next sc. Repeat from * around. Sl st in first sc. **RND 4** Repeat Row 2, but make 4 decs around toe with 2 sc between decs. **RND 5** Repeat Row 2, but make 3 decs around toe with 3 sc between decs. **RND 6** Mark center st on toe. Ch 1, turn and work sc around to 4th st from marker, sc in next st and dec in next st, then work off as one st, dc in next 3 sts and work off as one st, dec in next st and sc in next st, then work off as one st. Make sc to end, sl st in first sc. **RND 7** Mark center st on toe. Ch 1, turn. Sc in next 2 sts, dec over next 2 sts, then make sc around to 5th st from marker, sc and dc worked off as one st, sc around to 5th sc from end, dec over next 2 sts, sc in next 2 sts, sl st in first sc. **RND 8** Repeat Row 7. **RND 9** Repeat Row 9 omitting the dec around heel. **RND 10** Ch 1, sl st in each st. Fasten off.

Tongue: In MC, ch 4, 3 dc in first st. (Ch 3, turn. Dc in each dc of last rnd, 2 dc in end st) three times. Fasten off. Sl st in CC in first st, *ch 1, sl st in next dc, repeat from * to end. Fasten off. Sew in front opening.

Ties: Cut a length of CC about 75 inches long, double and work a ch. Fasten both ends to one side of slipper. Repeat for other side of slipper. Tie in bow.

Sweet Dreams SLIPPERS

Shown in color on page 4

These feminine-looking slippers with a scalloped edge and ankle tie are a perfect fit before settling down to sweet bedtime dreams.

Designed with Eskimo mukluks in mind, these slippers will keep your feet warm but also look pretty, too. And when you're looking good and feeling good, you're bound to have sweet dreams!

Directions are given for women's slippers in any length desired.

Materials: About 150 yards worsted weight yarn in main color (MC) and 100 yards in contrasting color (CC), a size K crochet hook and a size I crochet hook.

59

Finished Measurements: The slippers can be crocheted to any length desired.

Gauge: 3 dc and 2 rows equal 1 inch.

TO SAVE TIME, TAKE TIME TO CHECK GAUGE.

With MC and size K hook, ch 37. Dc in 3rd ch from hook and in each ch — 36 dc (count beginning ch as 1 sc), turn.

Eyelet Row: ROW 1 Change to size I hook, ch 3, dc in next dc, *ch 1, sk 1 dc, dc in next 2 dc, repeat from * across. Ch 3, turn. **ROWS 2 and 3** Dc in each st, turn. Drop yarn on last row, *do not fasten off.*

Instep: Join CC and work over center 18 dc only for 12 rows or until about 1 inch less than desired length.

Sides and Sole: Pick up MC. Ch 3, turn. Dc in each dc around ankle to instep; 2 dc over end dc of each row along instep; dc across toe, dec 1 dc at each side of center st; work across other edge of instep and ankle to correspond. Ch 3, turn.

For the next three rows, dc in dc around, dec 2, dc at toe as before. Fasten off.

Sew sole and heel seams.

Finishing: Work a shell row around top as follows: Join color as desired at top of heel, ch 3, (2 dc, sc) in same st, *sk 2 sts, (sc, 3 dc, sc) in next st, repeat from * around, join with sl st. Fasten off.

Tie Cord: With two strands, ch 80. Fasten off. Lace through eyelets.

Indian-Style
SLIPPERS

Styled after the soft leather Native American moccasins that are still popular today, these slippers have the added benefit of being washable.

Shown in color on page 6

The soles of these Indian-style slippers are worked in dark brown yarn, so they won't easily show dirt. But, even if they do, just throw the slippers in the washing machine, and they'll look like new.

Directions are given for women's size slippers. They're very stretchy and pliable, so one size fits all.

Materials: About 400 yards dark brown and gold worsted weight acrylic yarn, a size H crochet hook, a size F crochet hook and a tapestry needle.

Gauge: In sc with size F hook, 9 sts equal 2 inches.

TO SAVE TIME, TAKE TIME TO CHECK GAUGE.

Sole: With double strand of dark brown and size H hook, ch 25. **RND 1** 3 Sc in 2nd ch from hook, sc in each of next 10 chs, hdc in next 12 chs, 5 hdc in last ch; turn and work in back lps of ch; hdc in each of next 12 lps, sc in remaining 11 lps — 53 sts. **RND 2** 2 Sc in each of next 2 sts, sc in each of next 23 sts, 2 sc in each of next 5 sts, sc in remaining 23 sts — 60 sts. **RND 3** 2 Sc in next st, sc in next st, 2 sc in next st, sc in next 24 sts, (2 sc in next st, sc in next st) four times, 2 sc in next st, sc in each of next 24 sts — 67 sts. **RND 4** Sc in next 16 sts, hdc in next 12 sts, sc in next 15 sts, hdc in next 12 sts, sc in next 12 sts, sl st to first st of Rnd 4. Fasten off.

Sides and Back: RND 5 Join double strand of gold in back lp of sl st. With size H hook, ch 1. Sc in back lp of next st and back lp of each st around. Fasten off one strand of yarn. **RND 6** With single strand and size F hook, hdc in ch 1 and each st around. **RND 7** Hdc in each of next 31 sts, yo, insert hook in next st, yo and draw up a lp, yo, insert hook in next st, yo and draw up a lp, yo and pull through all 5 lps on hook at once (dec made), (hdc in each of next 2 sts, dec over next 2 sts) three times, hdc in next 22 sts — 63 sts. **RND 8** Hdc in next 31 sts, (dec over next 2 sts, hdc in next 2 sts) twice, dec over next 2 sts, hdc in next 22 sts — 60 sts. **RND 9** Hdc in next 31 sts, dec over next 2 sts, hdc in next 2 sts, dec over next 2 sts, hdc in next 23 sts — 58 sts. Fasten off.

Top of Foot: With single strand of gold and size F hook, ch 13. **ROW 1** Sc in 2nd ch from hook and each ch across — 12 sts. Ch 1, turn. **ROW 2** Sc in next st and each st across — 12 sts. Do not ch 1. Turn. **ROW 3** Sc in next st and each st across to within last st — 10 sts. Ch 1, turn. **ROW 4** Sc in next st and each st across — 10 sts. Do not ch 1. Turn. **ROW 5** Sc in next st and each st across to within last st — 8 sts. Ch 1, turn. **ROW 6** Sc in next st and each st across — 8 sts. Do not ch 1. Turn. **ROW 7** Sc in next st and each st across to within last st — 6

sts. Fasten off.

Insert top of slipper in place. Beginning at one of the top corners, with single strand of brown and size F hook, sc top to main part of slipper — one sc for each st of main slipper. Continue sc around side, back and other side of slipper until you are at your starting place. Now, sc across top of slipper, sl st to side. Ch 4, *sk next st, dc in next st, ch 1; repeat from * for side, back, other side and top. Sl st in 3rd ch. Sc in each st for side, back, other side and top. Fasten off.

Finishing: Weave in all ends. With single strand of gold and size F hook, make a ch about 26 inches long. Fasten off.

Thread one end of ch in tapestry needle and weave through dc. Tie bow in front.

Shown in color on page 3

Funny Bunny
FOOTWEAR

Warm, wearable bunny footwear fits babies to daddies and everyone in between. Knit a pair for the entire family, so everyone will have hares on their feet.

These bunny slippers are ideal for Easter gifts — fill them with treats instead of using the traditional basket. But fluffy little bunnies aren't just for Easter; big and little kids alike will enjoy them throughout the year.

Small, medium and large sizes are given for three different categories: child, youth and adult. Exact fit in each category can be achieved by adjusting length of the finished slipper.

Materials: About 175 (350, 525) yards worsted weight white or white-and-gray variegated yarn, small amount of white worsted weight yarn for tails, buttons for eyes and nose (or contrasting yarn to make French knots), thread for whiskers, number 9 knitting needles, scissors and a large tapestry needle.

Finished Measurements:
For child's sizes, width measures 2-1/2 inches with length of 5 inches (small); 5-1/2 inches (medium); and 6-inches (large). For youth sizes, width measures 2-3/4 inches with length of 7 inches (small); 7-1/2 inches (medium); and 8 inches (large.) For adult sizes, width measures 3 inches with length of 9 inches (small); 10-1/2 inches (medium); and 12 inches (large).

Gauge: With two strands of yarn in garter stitch, 4 stitches and 7 rows equal 1 inch.

TO SAVE TIME, TAKE TIME TO CHECK GAUGE.

Special Abbreviation: KFL (knit, forming loop) K1, but leave st on left needle, bring yarn forward between needles and wind over left thumb to form loop. Return yarn between needles to back (maintaining lp on thumb) and K the same st again, (two stitches formed on right needle). Bring first stitch over second as if to bind off.

Instructions are given in child's size small (youth and adult sizes follow in parentheses).

With double strand of yarn, cast on 23(29,35) sts.
ROW 1 *KFL, K1, repeat from * three (four, five) times, K7(9,11), **K1, KFL, repeat from ** three (four, five) times. **ROWS 2 and 4** *K7(9,11), P1, repeat from *, K7(9,11). **ROW 3** *K1, KFL, repeat from * two (three, four) times, K11(13,15), **KFL, K1, repeat from ** two (three, four) times. Repeat these four rows until piece measures 1-1/2 (2, 2-1/2)

inches less than the desired length, ending with an even row.

Toe Shaping: ROWS 1,3 and 5 *P1, K1, repeat from * across. **ROWS 2 and 4** *K1, P1, repeat from * across. (For youth sizes repeat Rows 2-5 once more; for adult sizes repeat Rows 2-5 twice more.) **ROW 6** P2 tog across, ending with P1—12(15,18) sts. **ROW 7** K2 tog across (for youth sizes end with K1)—6(8,9) sts. **ROW 8** P2 tog across (adult sizes end with P1) —three (four, five) sts.

Ears: (Make four.) Cast on 5(7,9) sts. **ROW 1** K. **ROW 2** Inc 1 (K in front and back of st), K to last st, inc 1. Repeat Rows 1 and 2 once more for child's sizes — 9 sts; twice more for youth sizes — 13 sts; and three times more for adult sizes — 17 sts.

NEXT ROW K2 tog, K to within last 2 sts, K2 tog. Repeat this row until 5(7,9) sts remain. Bind off. Work in ends of yarn and sew ears in place on top of slippers where toe ribbing begins.

Whiskers, Eyes, Nose: Cut six 3-(4-,5-) inch lengths of thread. Draw through front tip of slipper, knot in center and trim to even. Sew buttons in place for eyes and nose or create eyes and nose. *Note: To prevent a loose button from being accidentally swallowed, slippers intended for children under the age of three years should be finished with French knots for eyes and nose.*

Finishing: Make two small (medium, large) pom-poms from scraps of white yarn, sew to back of slippers.

Corn in the Morn SLIPPERS

Double thick sole, form-fitting back and popcorn stitch top make these corny slippers fun for little feet to wear.

A healthy breakfast is the best start a growing child can get each morning. These corny slippers are a perfect fit under the breakfast table, not to mention a wholesome role model for menu selection. Because they're made of cotton yarn, they won't make little toes too toasty, just cozy and comfortable enough to sit through the most important meal of the day.

Directions are given for a child's size small with medium and large sizes in parentheses.

Materials: About 220 yards green and yellow sport weight cotton yarn, number 5 knitting needles and a tapestry needle. Other yarn, such as 4-ply worsted weight acrylic yarn

Shown in color on page 9

can be substituted, but be certain to check your gauge.

Finished Measurements:
Length: 5-1/2(6-1/2,7-1/2)inches
Width: 2(2-1/2,3)inches
Gauge: With double strand of yarn, 4 sts and 9 rows equal one inch.

TO SAVE TIME, TAKE TIME TO CHECK GAUGE.

Special Abbreviation: PC (Popcorn Stitch) — K in front, back and front of st (3 sts formed), sl rightmost st over other two, sl next st over remaining st — 1 st remains.

Pattern is given in size small (medium, large following in parenthesis).

Sole: (Make four.) With green, cast on 4 (5, 6) sts. **ROW 1** P. **ROW 2** Inc 1 in first st (K in front and back of st), K to within last 2 sts, inc 1 in next st, K1. Repeat these two rows until there are 8 (9, 10) sts on needle. Continue working in stockinette st (P odd rows, K even rows) until work measures 2 (2-1/2, 3) inches from cast-on edge, ending with a K row. Repeat Rows 1 and 2 — 10(11,12) sts on needle. Continue working in stockinette st until work measures 5(6,7) inches from cast-on edge. **NEXT ROW** K1, K2 tog, K to within last 3 sts, sl 1, K1, psso, K1. **NEXT ROW** P. Repeat these 2 rows until there are 4(5,6) sts on needle, ending with a K row. Bind off in P.

Back Heel and Cuff: With green, cast on 3 sts. **ROW 1** K to within one st, inc 1 (K in front and back of st). **ROW 2** Inc one st in first st, K across.

Repeat Rows 1 and 2 until there are 11(12,13) sts on needle. **ROW 3** K to within last two sts, K2 tog. **ROW 4** K2 tog, K across. Repeat Rows 3 and 4 until there are 3 sts on needle. Bind off. Working along straight edge of triangle-shaped cuff, pick up and K 11(12,13) sts. **ROW 1** K across. **ROW 2** Inc 1 in first st, K to within last 2 sts, inc 1 in next st, K1. Repeat Rows 1 and 2 until there are 23(26,29) sts on needle, ending with Row 1. Bind off.

Front: With yellow cast on 4(6,8) sts. **ROW 1** *PC, K1, repeat from * across. **ROW 2** P. **ROW 3** *PC, K1, repeat from * across, cast on 2 sts at end of row. **ROW 4** P across, cast on 2 sts at end of row. Repeat Rows 1-4 until there are 12(14,16) sts on needle. **ROW 5** Repeat Row 1. **ROWS 6 and 8** P. **ROW 7** *PC, K1, repeat from * across. Repeat Rows 4-8 until work measures 5(6,7) inches from cast-on edge. Repeat Rows 5-7 once more. **NEXT ROW** P2 tog twice, P to within last 4 sts, P2 tog twice. Repeat Row 1. **LAST ROW** P2 tog across. Cast off.

Finishing: Place wrong (purl) sides of soles together, stitch around edges with green yarn. Center back heel and cuff perpendicular to back of sole, stitch in place with green yarn. At toe edge, center front and stitch to sole with yellow yarn; stitch up to second or third ridge of back edges. Leave only enough room for foot to slide in and out; slippers should fit snugly.

Shown in color on page 8

Lounging Slippers

A cup of tea, a good book and a quiet afternoon will go perfectly with these comfortable slippers — just right for lounging around.

Somewhat reminiscent of elfin boots, these lounging slippers will stay securely on your feet, whether or not you have them propped up. You'll love their over-the-ankle warmth, and the yarn ties are functional as well as ornamental.

Directions are given for adult size small, medium and large.

Materials: The size knitting needles used to make these slippers determine the slipper size. For small size, use numbers 6 and 8 needles; medium size, numbers 7 and 9 needles; large size, numbers 8 and 10 needles. You'll also need about 200 yards worsted weight yarn for main color (MC) and 200 yards worsted weight yarn for contrasting color (CC), a tapestry needle to weave seams and a size H crochet hook to make tie.

Finished Measurements:
Small: 7 inch length
Medium: 9 inch length
Large: 11 inch length
Gauge: Gauge will be different for each size.

Small: In stockinette on number 8 needles, 5 sts equal 1 inch.

Medium: In stockinette on number 9 needles, 4 sts equal 1 inch.

Large: In stockinette on number 10 needles, 3 sts equal 1 inch.

TO SAVE TIME, TAKE TIME TO CHECK GAUGE.

Cast on loosely 68 sts with number 8(9,10) needles and MC. **ROWS 1-2** K. **ROW 3** (Right Side) K1, inc 1, K27, inc 1, place marker on needle, K8, place marker on needle, inc 1, K27, inc 1, K1 — 72 sts. **ROWS 4, 6, 7, and 8** K. **ROW 5** K1, inc 1, K to one st before marker, inc one st, sl marker, K8, sl marker, inc one st, K to last 2 sts, inc one st, K1 — 76 sts. Fasten off. Join CC to continue. **ROW 9** K to 4 sts before marker, (sl 1, K1, psso) twice, sl marker, P2, K4, P2, sl marker, K2 tog twice, K to end of row. **ROW 10** K the K sts, P the P sts as they face you. **ROWS 11-18** Repeat Rows 9 and 10 four times — 56 at end of Row 18 sts. **ROW 19** K1, (sl 1, K1, psso) twice, K to 2 sts before marker, sl 1, K1, psso, P2, K4, P2, K2 tog, K to 5 sts from end, K2 tog twice, K1 — 50 sts. **ROW 20** P the P sts, K the K sts. **ROW 21** K to 2 sts before marker, sl 1, K1, psso, sl marker, P2, K4, P2, sl marker, K2 tog, K to end of row. **ROW 22** P the P sts and K the K sts as they face you. **ROWS 23-32** Repeat Rows 21 and 22 five times — 38 sts at end of Row 32. Fasten off light yarn, join dark yarn for eyelet row. **ROW 33** (Eyelet Row) With size 6(7,8) needles, *K2, yo, K2 tog, repeat from * across row, ending with yo, K2. **ROW 34** (Work yo as sts in K or P as they fall) Work in K1, P1 ribbing, ending P1 — 39 sts. **ROW 35** K1, *P1, K1, repeat from * across. **ROWS 36-39** Repeat Rows 33 and 34 twice. Bind off loosely, with large size needles.

Finishing: Weave back and sole seams together, matching rows, weave in all ends.

Crochet a chain or twist a double cord, one strand of each color, 26 inches long.

Weave cord through eyelets, fastening in bow at front of slipper.

Slender Silhouette
SLIPPERS

Narrow-width feet will enjoy the comfortable fit of these slender slippers designed in sizes for children as well as adult men and women.

Shown in color on page 9

The slim contours of these easy-to-make slippers assure that they will give a comfort- able fit, especially for nar- row feet. If other knit or crocheted slippers are too loose and create gaps when worn, then this pattern may be just the answer you need.

Directions are for children's slippers with changes for women's and men's sizes in parentheses.

Materials: 200 (325, 450) yards worsted weight yarn and a size H crochet hook.

Gauge: 3 sc equal one inch at instep.

TO SAVE TIME, TAKE TIME TO CHECK GAUGE.

Ch 2. **RND 1** Work 8 (10,14) sc in first ch, join with sl st (toe). *Note: Always ch 1 to turn at end of each row.* **RND 2** 2 Sc in next sc, sc in next 3(4,6) sc, 2 sc in next sc, sc in next 3(4,6) sc.

NEXT 6(8,12) RNDS Work in sc, making inc over inc of previous rnd — 2 inc sts made each rnd.

Work even in sc until instep is length desired.

Fold toe so inc points form edges or sides of foot, sc across to top center of instep. ch 1, turn.

Work even in sc rows until heel is length desired. Sew heel seam.

Bathtime BOOTS

Treat your feet to a refreshing bubble bath, followed by a soothing application of moisturizer and then let them luxuriate in these soft, comfy boots.

Bath salts, a pumice stone and a bottle of fragrant lotion would be the perfect accompaniment to tuck inside these slippers for an extra special gift. With plenty of room at the top to slip a foot into, the slippers nevertheless stay snugly in place while you are wearing them.

Directions are given for child's 7-inch sole, with ladies 8-inch sole and men's 10-inch sole in parentheses.

Materials: About 240 yards purple (A), 240 yards magenta (B) and 160 yards variegated (C) worsted weight yarn; a size H crochet hook for child's size; and a size I crochet hook for adult sizes.

Finished Measurements:
Child: 7 inches long
Women: 8 inches long
Men: 10 inches long

Gauge: In sc, 4 sts and 3 rows equal 1 inch.

TO SAVE TIME, TAKE TIME TO CHECK GAUGE.

Sole: With A, ch 20 (24,30), 3 sc in 2nd ch from hook. **RND 1** Sc in each of next 8(10,13) sts, hdc in next st, dc in each of next 8(10,13) sts, 5 dc in end ch. Along other side of ch, dc in 8(10,13) sts, hdc in next st, sc in 8(10,13) sts, sc in same st where first 3 sts were made, sl st. **RND 2** Ch 1,

2 sc in each of next 2 sc, sc in each st to 5 dc sts (in toe), 2 sc in each of the 5 dc, sc in each st to beginning, sl st. **RND 3** Ch 1, 2 sc in next sc, sc in next st, 2 sc in next st, sc in each st to 2 sc at tip of toe, *2 sc in next sc, sc in next sc, repeat from * four times, sc to ch 1, sl st. **RND 4** Ch 1, sc in next sc, 2 sc in next sc, sc in next sc, 2 sc in next sc, sc in each sc to st over hdc in first rnd, hdc, dc in next 11(13,15) sc, *2 dc in next sc, dc in next sc, repeat from * four times, dc in next 11(13,15) sc, hdc, sc to ch 1, sl st — 64 sts. **RND 5** Ch 1, sc in front lp of each sc around sole (edge of sole). **RND 6** Ch 1, sc in each sc around sole, sl st.

RND 7 — **Top:** Join C, sc in each sc around, sl st.

RND 8 *Sc in first sc, sk next sc, putting hook horizontally under next sc in second row below, tr. Repeat from * around sole, join. **RND 9** Join B, sc in each sc around, sl st. **RND 10** (Dec Rnd) Ch 2, hdc in 30 sts, draw up a lp in each of next 4 sts, take off all lps at one time, ch 1 tightly (dec made), hdc over 30 sts. **RND 11** Repeat Rnd 10, dec over center 6 sts. **RNDS 12, 13 and 14** Repeat Rnd 10, dec over center 8 sts. **RNDS 15, 16 and 17** Hdc in each st, sl st at end of each rnd. **RNDS 18 and 19** Join A, sc in each st, sl st at end of each rnd. **RND 20** Join C, sc in each st, sl st. **RND 21** Repeat Row 8. **RND 22** Join A, sc in each sc around. Fasten off.

Pink Poodle
SLIPPERS

*Anyone who remembers
owning a poodle skirt,
wearing her hair in a pony
tail and playing with a hula
hoop will enjoy a pair of
these slippers.*

Pink poodles weren't the
only thing that was all the
rage back in the '50s, but
they were definitely part of the
"in" crowd. Someone you know
who lived through those
"happy days" would no doubt
love a pair of these nostalgic
pink poodle slippers —
wouldn't you?

Directions are given for
women's slippers in any length
desired.

Materials: About 325 yards

Shown in color on page 8

pink (MC) and 20 yards black (CC) worsted weight yarn, a tapestry needle and sizes G and H crochet hooks.

Finished Measurements: The slippers can be crocheted to any length desired.

Gauge: 4 sc equal 1 inch; 4 rows equal 1 inch.

TO SAVE TIME, TAKE TIME TO CHECK GAUGE.

Soles: With size H hook and two strands MC, ch 2. **ROW 1** In 2nd ch from hook, work 3 sc. Ch 1, turn. **ROW 2** Work 2 sc in next sc, sc in next sc, 2 sc in remaining sc — 5 sts. Ch 1, turn. **ROW 3** Sc in next sc, sc in next 3 sc, 2 sc in remaining sc — 7 sc. Ch 1, turn. **ROW 4** Work even. **ROW 5** Ch 1, turn. Sc in same st, sc in next 5 sc, 2 sc in remaining sc — 9 sts. Ch 1, turn. **ROW 6** Work even. **ROW 7** Ch 1, turn. 2 sc in next st, sc in next 6 sc, 2 sc in last sc — 11 sts. Ch 1, turn. **ROWS 8-20** Work even. **ROW 21** Dec 1 sc at each end, working middle sts in sc — 9 sts. Work even until 1/2 inch short of desired length. **NEXT ROW** Dec 1 sc each end, working middle sts in sc — 7 sts. **NEXT ROW** Work even. **NEXT ROW** Dec one sc each end, working middle sts in sc — 5 sts. Fasten off.

Top: Starting at toe, ch 2. **ROW 1** Work 5 sc in 2nd ch from hook. Ch 1, turn. **ROW 2** 2 sc in first sc, *sc in next sc, 2 sc in next sc, repeat from * — 8 sc. Ch 1, turn. **ROW 3** Sc in first 2 sc, *2 sc in next sc, sc in next 2 sc, repeat from * — 10 sc. Ch 1, turn. **ROW 4** 2 sc in first sc, sc in each sc to last sc, 2 sc in last sc — 12 sc. Ch 1, turn. **ROWS 5 and 6** Sc in each sc. Ch 1, turn. **ROW 7** Sc in first 3 sc, 2 sc in next sc, sc in next 4 sc, 2 sc in next sc, sc in last 3 sc — 14 sc. Ch 1, turn. **ROW 8** Repeat Row 6. **ROWS 9-14** Repeat Rows 4, 5 and 6 twice — 18 sc. **ROW 15** Make 2 sc in the 4th, 8th, 11th and 15th sc — 22 sc. **ROWS 16, 17 and 18** Work even.

Side Piece: Work first 7 sc. Ch 1, turn. Work these sts, inc one st at inner edge every 4th row four times. Work even on 11 sc until piece will reach to center back of sole. Fasten off.

Sk center 8 sc, join yarn in next sc, ch 1, sc in same sc and next 6 sc.

Work other side piece to correspond.

Ears: (Make four.) Starting at tip, ch 4. **ROW 1** Sc in 2nd ch from hook and each ch across — 3 sc. Ch 1, turn. **ROW 2** Sc in first sc, 2 sc in next sc, sc in last sc — 4 sc. Ch 1, turn. **ROW 3** Inc in first and last sc — 6 sc. **ROWS 4-12** Work even. **ROWS 13, 14 and 15** Sk first sc, sc in each remaining sc — 3 sc remain. Fasten off.

Finishing: Fold top of ears lengthwise and sew to corners of instep. Embroider ears and nose with black yarn and tapestry needle.

Wind yarn 50 times over four fingers. Tie securely at center, clip loops and sew to edge of instep. Sew sole to upper of slipper.

Shown in color on page 10

Midnight Snack Attack
SLIPPER-SOCKS

The midnight snacker will be able to tip-toe quietly to the kitchen in these slipper-socks without waking anyone during a nocturnal forage for food.

Some folks are concerned enough about their waistlines to say "no" to second helpings at dinner. Their resolution may even allow them to turn down a rich dessert. But late at night the snack attack hits, and they have to sneak downstairs for an old-fashioned mile-high Dagwood Bumstead sandwich.

With these slipper-socks, at least they won't catch a cold when the late night snack attack strikes.

These adult slipper-socks can be knit to any length desired.

Materials: About 325 yards worsted weight yarn and number 8 knitting needles.

Finished Measurements: The slipper socks can be knit to any length desired.

Gauge: 8-1/2 sts equal 2 inches in stockinette.

TO SAVE TIME, TAKE TIME TO CHECK GAUGE.

Lower Section: Cast on 16 sts and work in K1, P1 ribbing for 2 inches. **ROW 1** (Right Side) K1, yo, K across to last st, yo, K1. **ROW 2** (Wrong Side) P across. Repeat Rows 1 and 2 until there are 34 sts, ending with a wrong side row.

Shape Heel: ROW 1 K22, sl 1 as-if-to-knit, K1, psso, leave remaining sts. **ROW 2** Sl 1 as-if-to-purl, P10, P2 tog. **ROW 3** Sl 1 as-if-to-purl, K10, sl 1 as-if-to-knit, K1, psso. Repeat Rows 2 and 3 alternately until 16 sts remain, ending with a wrong-side row. P the 2 remaining sts on left needle.

Sole: Work in stockinette (K one row, P one row) over these 16 sts until sole is length desired.

Shape Toe: With right side facing, K1, sl 1 as-if-to-knit, K1, psso, K across to last 3 sts, K2 tog, K1. **NEXT ROW** (Wrong Side) P across. Repeat these 2 rows until 10 sts remain, ending with a P row. Bind off.

Upper Section: Cast on 24 sts and work in K1, P1 ribbing for 2 inches. Work in stockinette until piece measures the same as sole.

Shape Toe: Work same as for lower section until 14 sts remain on needle, ending with a wrong side row. **NEXT ROW** K1, sl 1 as-if-to-knit, K2 tog, psso, K across to last 4 sts, K3 tog, K1. **NEXT ROW** P across. Bind off. Sew toe seams on reverse side, using running back stitch. Sew side seams on right side, using flat stitch. Steam press lightly on wrong side.

FOOT COZIES

Knit rows and rows of cables without actually using a cable needle with this pair of pretty slippers that will fit your feet quite cozily.

If you like the look of knitted cables but are hesitant to try patterns that call for them, this design is for you!

Shown in color on page 3

Directions are given for women's size small/medium with size large in parentheses.

Materials: About 500 yards worsted weight yarn, number 9 knitting needles, a size G crochet hook and stitch markers.

Finished Measurements:

Small/Medium: 7 inches long

Large: 8-1/2 inches long

Gauge: In stockinette stitch, 4 sts equal 1 inch.

TO SAVE TIME, TAKE TIME TO CHECK GAUGE.

Sole: With double strand of yarn, cast on

46(50) sts. **ROW 1** P23 (25), place marker on needle, P to end of row. **ROW 2** (K1, inc 1 in next st) twice, K to within 4 sts of marker, in each of next 8 sts, K to within 4 sts of end, (inc 1 in next st, K1) twice — 58(62) sts. **ROW 3** P. **ROW 4** (K1, inc one st in next st) twice, K to within 4(6) sts of marker, inc in each of next 8(12) sts, K to within 4 sts of end, (inc 1 in next st, K1) twice —70(78) sts. **ROW 5** P. **ROWS 6 and 7** K (Turning ridge formed).

Pattern Rows 8-11: **ROW 8** P2, *K2, P2, repeat from * across. **ROW 9** K2, *P2, K2, repeat from * ending with K2. **ROW 10** *P2, K2 tog (leaving sts on left-hand needle), K first st again (the one that is now at the end of left-hand needle), sl both sts from needle, repeat from * ending with P2. **ROW 11** Repeat Row 9. **ROWS 12-15** Repeat Rows 8-11. **ROWS 16-18** Repeat Rows 8-10. **ROW 19** (Wrong Side) Work 18 sts in pattern, *P2 tog, K2 tog, repeat from * seven (nine) times, P2 tog, work remaining 18 sts in pattern. **ROW 20** *K2 tog, yo, repeat from * across, ending K1. Bind off remaining 53(57) sts.

Finishing: Sew bottom of sole and back seam. With sole facing and single strand of yarn, work 1 row sc around sole in turning ridge. Crochet cord as follows: With double strand, ch 30 inches. Fasten off, weave in ends. Knot each end and draw through yo holes. Tie bow in front.

HIGH-TOP BOOTIES

Baby booties never looked like these, but you'll love the fit of these tiny high-toppers. They stay put on even the most active little feet.

These cute and practical booties are sized corresponding to actual shoe sizes and fastened with regular shoe laces. Directions are given for size 1 (0-3 months) with sizes 2 (3-6 months), 3 (6-9 months), 4 (9-12 months) and 5 (12 - 15 months) in parentheses. You may want to read through the instructions a few times and highlight the directions that apply to the size you're making before you begin knitting.

Materials: About 160 yards red, white and blue sport weight yarn; number 5 knitting needles; a pair of

18-inch dress shoe laces for sizes 1 and 2; and a pair of 24-inch length dress shoe laces for sizes 3, 4 and 5.

Finished Measurements: Length of Sole: 3-1/2 (4, 4-1/2, 5, 5-1/2) inches

Width of Sole: 2(2,2-1/4, 2-1/4, 2-1/4) inches

Height at Back of Ankle: 2-3/4 (2-3/4, 3-1/2, 3-1/2, 3-1/2) inches

Gauge: 11 sts and 16 rows equal 2 inches in stockinette stitch (K one row, P one row); 11 sts and 24 rows equal 2 inches in garter stitch (K every row).

TO SAVE TIME, TAKE TIME TO CHECK GAUGE.

Special Abbreviations: SKP (slip, knit, passover) — This decrease is worked as follows. Slip one stitch as-if-to-knit from the left-hand to the right-hand needle. Knit next stitch. Pass over by taking the tip of the left-hand needle and lifting the slipped stitch up and over the knitted stitch and off the end of the right-hand needle.

Lower Body of Slipper: With blue, cast on 50(56, 62,66,72) sts marking the center 6 sts of cast-on row. Working in garter st, K four rows. With white, K two rows. Cut white, leaving a 3-inch tail. With blue, K three rows.

Divide for Top of Toe/ Tongue: (Wrong Side) With blue, K14(15,17, 18,19), sl the sts just knitted (found on right-hand needle) to stitch holder, bind off 8(10,11,12,14) sts, K6, sl the 6 sts found on right-hand needle to stitch holder, bind off

8(10,11,12,14) sts, K14 (15,17,18,19). Cut blue, leaving a 6-inch tail for seaming.

With wrong side facing you and beginning at outer edge, sl the first 14(15,17,18,19) sts onto end of the needle — 28(30,34,36,38) sts.

Ankle: ROW 1 (Right Side) With white and outside of slipper facing you, K across row joining sides of ankle. **ROW 2** (Wrong Side) Cast on 2 sts at end of needle. Beginning with 2 sts just cast on, K3, P26 (28,32,34,36), K1 — 30 (32,36,38,40) sts. **ROW 3** Cast on 2 sts at end of needle. Beginning with cast on sts, K across all sts — 32 (34,38,40,42) sts. **ROWS 4, 6, 8, 10, 12, 14 and 16** K3, P until 3 sts remain, K3. **ROW 5** (Eyelet and Dec Row) K2 tog, yo, K1,

SKP, K8(9,11,12,13), K2 tog, K2, SKP, K8(9,11, 12,13), K2 tog, K1, yo, K2 tog— 28(30,34,36,38) sts. **ROW 7** K across. **ROW 9** (Eyelet and Dec Row) K2 tog, yo, K1, SKP, K6(7,9, 10,11), K2 tog, K2, SKP, K6(7,9,10,11), K2 tog, K1, yo, K2 tog — 24 (26,30, 32,34) sts. **ROW 11** K across. **ROW 13** (Eyelet and Dec Row) K2 tog, yo, K1, SKP, K until 5 sts remain, K2 tog, K1, yo, K2 tog — 22(24,28,30,32) sts. *Note: For sizes 1 and 2 only, skip rows 14-17 and work border.* **ROW 15** (Sizes 3,4 and 5 only) K across. **ROW 17** Repeat Row 13 — 26(28,30) sts. Work border.

Border: K three rows even. Bind off all sts as if to knit. Fasten off.

Upper Toe: Sl the 6 sts from stitch holder onto

needle. With red, work in stockinette stitch, inc one st each side every other row two (two, three, three, three) times — 10(10, 12, 12,12) sts. Work even until upper toe measures 1-1/2 (1-3/4, 2, 2, 2-1/4) inches from joining, ending with a K row.

Tongue: ROW 1 K2, P6 (6,8,8,8), K2. **ROW 2** K across. Repeat Rows 1 and 2 for 1-3/4 (1-3/4, 2-1/4, 2-1/4, 2-1/4) inches from first row of tongue, ending with Row 2. K three rows in garter st and then bind off as if to knit.

Sole: With red and right side of toe facing you, pick up 6 sts using the back lps of the sts marked on cast-on row. Knit across row. Working in garter st and joining sole to lower body each row as you work (optional

— see detailed instructions below) inc one st each side next and every other row two (two, three, three, three) times — 10(10,12,12,12) sts. Work even for 30(36,38,42,44) rows — 34(40,44,48,50) rows total. Dec one st each side next and every other row two (two, three, three, three) times. Bind off as-if-to-knit.

Joining Sole to Lower Body: You may join sole to lower body by sewing it to lower body after it is knitted or in the following manner as you work. At the end of each row, pick up a st in next closest inside loop of cast-on row onto right-hand needle with other sts of sole. At the beginning of next row, K2 tog (st picked up and first st of sole).

Finishing: Sew center

back seam of lower body of booties joining edges of garter st rows. Graft bound off edge of sole to lower body at back of heel or join sole to lower body if not joined as you knit.

Sew upper toe to bound-off edges of lower body. Weave in ends. Thread shoe lace through yo eyelets on slanted edges. Repeat directions for remaining slipper.

Crochet Slipper Patterns for Children

Crochet Slipper Patterns for Women

Crochet Slipper Patterns for Men

Knit Slipper Patterns for Children

Other Books From
THE CLASSIC COLLECTION

TATTING PATTERNS $6.95

COLLARS TO KNIT AND CROCHET $6.95

AFGHANS TO CROCHET $7.95

U.S. STATE QUILT BLOCKS $6.95

THE COMPLETE BOOK OF JIFFY NEEDLE TATTING $18.95

JIFFY NEEDLE TATTING, FROM A TO Z $8.95

JIFFY NEEDLE TATTING, QUICK & EASY $8.95

JIFFY NEEDLE TATTING, EXCITING FASHION ACCESSORIES $8.95

JIFFY NEEDLE TATTING, HOLIDAY COLLECTION $8.95

MORE GREAT AFGHANS $9.95

WARM & WEARABLE $9.95

LOVELY LACES (LARGE PRINT) $9.95

BOUTIQUE BONANZA (LARGE PRINT) $9.95

STITCHIN' TIME $9.95

HEIRLOOM QUILTS $24.95

DOILIES AND DAINTIES (LARGE PRINT) $9.95

Your Choice

of One of These

4 Popular Pattern Packets

Crochet Slippers for Little Nippers
WBS1128 $6.95

Knit Fruit Sachets
WBS1159 $6.95

Cross Stitch Baby Bunnies
WBS1131 $6.95

12 Projects in 1 pk

A Whole Year of Crafts
WBS1186 $6.95

MasterCard, VISA, Discover and American Express Credit Card Orders Call Toll-Free 1-800-678-8025

Use This Form to Order Your Free Pattern Packet and to Purchase Other Classic Patterns and Classic Collection Books

Item #	Description	Qty.	Price
	(Your Choice)	1	FREE
	Total for Books and Products		
	Shipping and Handling		$3.00
	Missouri Residents Add 6% tax, Iowa Residents 5%		
	Total Enclosed		

Name

Address

City

State and Zip

Place order form in envelope and mail to:

WORKBASKET Books and Products, Dept. B95
P.O. Box 11230
Des Moines, IA 50340